Inventions Help People

by Stanley Brown

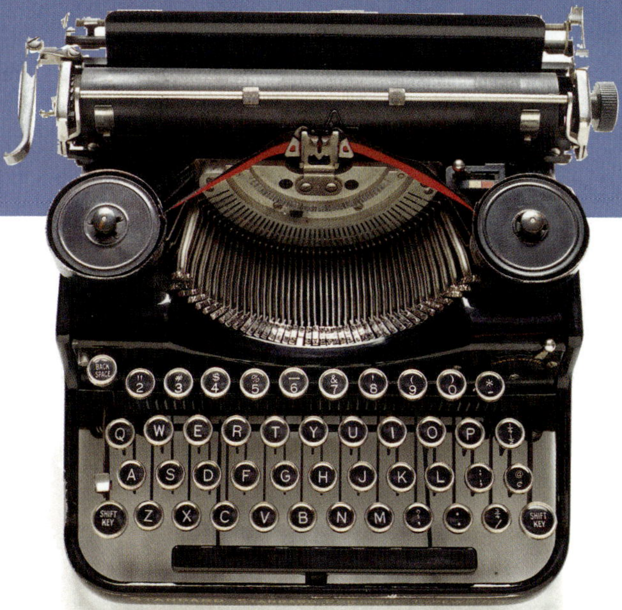

Glenview, Illinois • Boston, Massachusetts • Chandler, Arizona
Upper Saddle River, New Jersey

Inventors watch people do jobs.
They watch people have fun.
They think of better ways to do things.

washboard

washing machine

People used to wash clothes with washboards.

About 100 years ago, inventors made washing machines.

They are much easier to use.

People used to write only by hand.
Their hands got tired.
Sometimes ink from their pens made
a mess.

typewriter

About 140 years ago, inventors made typewriters.
Then writing was easier.
Today, writing is even easier.
People use computers.

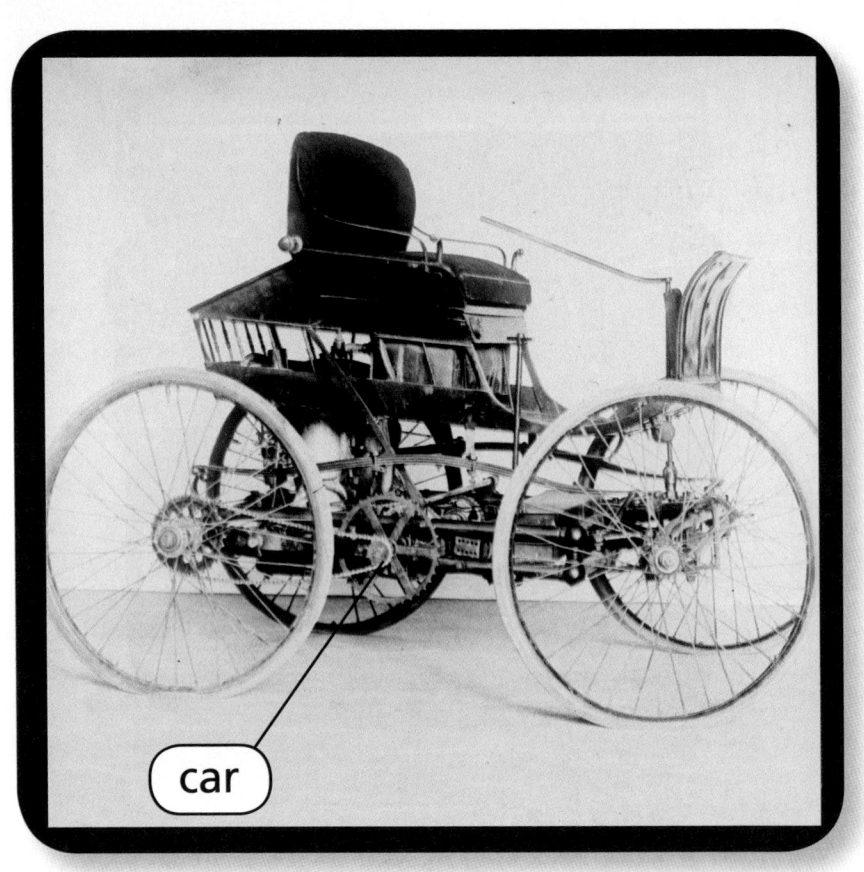

car

People used to walk to places.
They also rode horses or trains.
About 120 years ago, inventors
made cars.
The first cars were slow.

cars

Today cars are faster.
Sometimes there are many cars on the road.
Then cars move slowly.

basketball

kite

Some inventions are for fun. Basketball was invented about 115 years ago. Kites were invented more than 3,000 years ago.

What inventions do you like most?